Cash Flow

Ideas

for

Business Growth

How to Manage your
Cash Flow for
Small Business Growth

By

Dannis B. Moore

Disclaimer

Copyright©by Dannis B. Moore 2023.

Book Review

Cash flow ideas for business growth addresses the significance of spending, budgeting, saving and how to stay out of debt. Because improper management of finances and spendings can lead to debt.

Which might cause depression and high blood pressure with so many related issues. This book unveils steps on how you can reduce your spending, enabling you to save and budget your finances. As many people who read this book and study it, will understand practical knowledge on how to enhance business growth and activate cash flow ideas.

About the Author

The author of Cash Flow Ideas for Business Growth, Dannis B. Moore, is hailed as a major figure in the human potential movement. In this book, which has fundamental base knowledge on how to control your cash flow for business growth and recovery. He explains how you can properly spend, save and budget your money without being affected and traumatic.

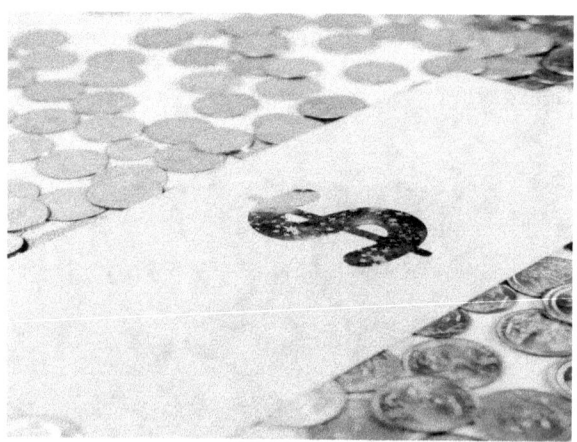

Table of Contents

Introduction

This book will help you realise that your present belief about business growth and financing is preventing you from moving forward.

You can choose to adopt a more helpful knowledge and practical steps or method of controlling your cash flow focusing and keeping a sound flow of income and expenditures with technical tactics to awaken your finances and experience business growth, Planning your funds so you can take full responsibility for your life.

Understanding cash flow ideas will help you avoid a similar potential immobility brought on by the debt caused by rapid spending and continually replacing constricting ideas with helpful ones to produce verifiable financial rewards.

Hence, it is beneficial to facilitate by measuring a shift that will improve your business growth from scratch with cash flow ideas contrasting prevalent limiting ideas and excesses that obstruct building a financial foundation with beliefs that encourage financial success.

This book states cash flow ideas, why you should Improve your finances and business growth with cash flow possibility, Because only few are capable of managing their finances.

Every day individuals all over the globe have their methods for keeping tabs on their expenditures.

The advice you'll receive here doesn't end with that! Hence, let's set you down the road to financial and business growth with various means of and insights to learn better ways of taking care of your finances.

CASH FLOW

CHAPTER 1

Setting Yourself Up for Change

"If we don't adapt, we won't advance. We are not living if we don't grow.

Conditioning exercises are a part of many workout programs because they help the body adapt to new muscular motions and cognitive demands. Similarly, an effective program for preparing for financial fitness includes actions that lessen the discomforts associated with financial situations. Reaching for a better financial situation also offers plenty of opportunities for resistance because it drives ongoing internal and external changes.

Even if they desire their lives to improve, the plurality of people striving for riches is resistant to change because they find solace in their relatively predictable financial patterns.

But they find financial freedom and satisfaction because they are reluctant to put up with short-term discomfort. Thankfully, you may progressively modify the ingrained attitudes, convictions, emotions, and behaviours holding you in your present financial situation by comprehending the causes of your resistance and actively planning for change.

Threats Indicated by the Identity Factor

One of the causes of resistance is what you dubbed the Identity Factor, a defence mechanism that safeguards an individual's sense of self and place in the universe.

The Identity Factor is frequently activated by changing financial situations, which can quickly endanger.

People usually avoid making the needed adjustments when this happens or fall back on old habits, protecting their comfortable lifestyle at all costs for fear that when the changes ultimately come about, they would make them feel uncomfortable, frightened, and confused.

The potential discomforts brought on by chance were unknown. She was paying off her debt and developing sound financial practices.

Developed a strategy to pay off her debt, quit using credit cards, and maintain better financial records with the aid of a credit counsellor.

She adhered to the program religiously for three months and was thrilled with the development she observed; but, in the fourth month, she started falling behind on her payments and twice had to borrow money from a friend.

She quit keeping a budget out of embarrassment, and six months later, she was right back where she had left off with more debt, a tendency to put off taking care of money matters, and a confused understanding of her spending.

Celine was upset with herself for impeding her advancement when she initially called me.

Once she understood she had been protecting her old identity, she realised her actions were not self-sabotaging but self-protective. She had protected her identity by resorting to behaviours with more predictable outcomes.

Over time, she learned how to work through the discomfort imposed by changed behaviours and began to develop, all of which helped her recommit to her financial plan.

Along with threatening someone's self-concept, significant change can also affect peer and family-of-origin relationships.

Since people know you as the person you once were, any change in your attitudes or behaviours requires them to respond to you differently and consequently undergo a change of their own.

Unchangeable friends or family members may attempt to obstruct your advancement, which increases your misery by making you think you are alone.

Thankfully, as you prepare for change, you'll realise that being alone is not inescapable.

You can re-analyze previous friendships and familiarities, as well as forge new bonds with others who mirror your evolving self and who will inevitably enter your life.

Acknowledging the Moving Dumbers It can be confusing to start a transition to a new financial position and behaviours at first because the path and results are both unpredictable. You have probably encountered what

I refer to as the "moving stupids" if you have ever relocated from one place to another.

Symptom

Feeling overburdened, bewildered, alone, and lost are among the symptoms, as is the propensity to lose things or choose foolishly.

Yet as you become adjusted to your new surroundings after moving into a new home, the discomforts it causes spending habits progressively improve.

It is possible to shorten the duration of the moving stupids and advance by accepting them as a sign of progress toward a new financial situation. He prepared to reevaluate his relationship with money when he was fifty years old.

Even though he wanted financial security, he felt his debt and was ashamed of his lack of financial knowledge. promised to cease using his credit cards when he started working with me, adhere to a spending plan we created, and keep a record of every penny he spent.

I've got a terrible case of the moving stupids, he complained. I'm so worried that I'll miscalculate and overspend.

Also, it feels like someone else is in my body as I write down my daily expenses. I don't usually act like this. informed me at the end of another two weeks that the confusion and uncertainty were progressively fading and that his new habits seemed more natural.

Yet, he experienced brief moments of confusion whenever he adopted a new practice, such as saving money from each paycheck.

But he was prepared to go through the experience because he knew the moving stupids were a sign of growth and would soon stop.

Actions

By increasing your self-awareness, the following acts can assist in overcoming resistance and prepare you for change. You make improvements and exercise patience.

Before attempting alterations, adjust to smaller ones to redouble your efforts.

1. Create a Prosperity Journal

To define your current status and monitor your development as you strengthen your financial muscles, Use it to express your feelings about change, write down your anxieties or reluctance, acknowledge your accomplishments, and highlight any questions that come to mind.

A later study of your findings is made comfortable by dating each entry.

2. Find a Prosperity Buddy

Working with a friend can improve your motivation to reduce discomfort and make the transition to a new financial position more joyful.

Choose a person you feel comfortable sharing personal information with at a specific frequency for your experience-sharing sessions, such as once or twice per week for a session.

Take turns throughout each one discussing the discomforts you've felt, such as alienation or disorientation, marking the progress you've made since the last session, asking for criticism if you'd like, and announcing what you'll do before the next session. Don't criticise your friend's actions or offer unsolicited advice because doing so could cause tension.

Instead, support your friend by highlighting their accomplishments. Choosing prosperity pals outside your partnership is a fantastic option for couples, especially if your financial discussions are frequently emotional.

You and your partner can work through your financial problems together, but having a third party as a confidant will likely inspire you to be more open and honest about problems. Those employing the buddy system advance faster than those who do not.

A rare technique, discussing financial behaviour offers new channels for individuals to express themselves authentically and frequently alleviates significant embarrassment related to financial behaviours.

3. Identify your Financial Self.

Your thoughts, beliefs, feelings, actions, and relationship with money make up your financial identity.

A clear understanding of your financial identity can help you spot warning signs of resistance to change in your finances and deal with the confusion that is likely to arise as your financial situation improves. In your prosperity diary, outline each element of your financial identity as you understand it while leaving space for future updates.

You can learn a lot about your financial situation by paying attention to the recurrent "I" comments you make, such as I'll never make enough money.

4. Make One Adjustment Externally.

You can adjust to new financial behaviours by consciously changing a small behaviour and observing your inner reactions. These are some potential outcomes:

• Position your toothbrush somewhere else.

• To get to a place you usually visit, choose a new street.

• Get up sooner than usual or go to bed a little later.

• Change your news station.

• Purchase a magazine that you have never seen before.

• Switch out one serving of cake or ice cream for a wholesome snack.

• Attend a meeting that has been on your mind.

• In your bathroom, turn the toilet paper roll around.

Once you feel at ease with the new action, practise it. Keep an eye out for any symptoms of confusion and how long it takes you to adjust to the shift in total.

While some people's discomfort only lasts a few days, others may experience it for weeks.

As you begin more new habits, you will forecast with some precision how long the identified risks and moving stupids will last once you have found your pace.

5. Change One Financial Behaviour.

Consider how you manage your money to prepare yourself for financial development. These are some potential outcomes:

• Keep a running tally of your daily earnings and outgoings.

• Pay the bills each week on time.

• Put an end to using your preferred credit card.

Even if it's just $3 every week, save the money you would have spent.

• Distribute a little cash.

• Practise frugal living for one day.

Watch out for your emotions when you make this adjustment, and note them in your prosperity diary. If you are experiencing discomfort, for the time being, write it down.

6. Look for any reluctance to make financial changes.

If you struggled to take the above step, ponder the following:

• Will changing my financial situation alter how I feel about myself?

• What do I fear will occur if I succeed financially? Will having financial security affect my view of who I am? Will it change how I interact with my family? Would being prosperous mean betraying a friend or possibly a family member?

7. Use a Utterances

The subconscious mind believes and exploits these beliefs to produce the desired results. Your subconscious mind will manifest opportunities for you if you tell it that life offers opportunities; conversely, if you tell it that you never receive what you desire.

Contradictory ideas, however, as well as unwillingness to change, can produce interference.

For instance, no matter how often I tell my subconscious mind that I have an easy cash flow if I simultaneously hold the contradictory notion that it is difficult for me to produce money.

Likewise, any discomfort I may feel due to the consequences of an easy financial flow, including dread.

CHAPTER 2

Establishing Realistic Objectives.

A personal trainer can create a bodybuilding routine to help reach their specific performance objectives.

In a similar vein, well-thought-out financial goals aid in the development of a person's strategy for achieving them.

Financial goals, first and foremost, have a description timely enough to direct financial habits.

For instance, setting a plan to pay off a twenty thousand dollar credit card debt within a year might encourage you to limit your purchases to things. As a result, you would decline if presented with the chance to purchase something on credit at a high price.

Setting a goal to double your income in two years could motivate you.

Personal Values.

Because these outcomes will make you feel truly fulfilled at every stage of the process, basing your goals on boosts your chances of achieving them.

Additionally, when you climb a financial ladder you have built for yourself rather than being imported from your spouse, friends, neighbours, or family, Success depends on how much money you have saved up and how many of your dreams have come true.

It's a good idea to become acutely aware of your values and health, way of life, relationships, career, education, and the welfare of all humanity.

Do you value simplicity, quality time with family, or giving back to your community through volunteer work?. Being mindful of your value and pursuing goals may overshadow your enjoyment.

As you grow financially, your chances of satisfying both your internal and exterior requirements increase if you prioritise your values and base your income goals on those you regard as non-negotiable.

Financial Goals That Are Practical.

Overcoming the subconscious goal-setting also demands a good dose of realism. If left to its own devices, a subconscious target and financial pattern will set its sights on a quantity of money so impractical that no real strategy for progress can emerge.

Worse yet, the inaction that follows tends to solidify the emotional theme of deprivation, trapping the person in a dysfunctional cycle. Realistic goals are to reduce the possibility of such a happening and promote a workable action plan.

By just acknowledging your debt, you may be able to take advantage of options like working with a professional or negotiating reduced credit card interest rates. You might opt to take a part-time job to earn some more cash. Little may prevent you from reaching your goals if you have a sincere desire to lower your debt and a set of attainable objectives in place. The same holds for plans to improve your income, savings, investments, or your ability to buy a new house. A greater level of comfort and the possibility of longer-lasting outcomes result from this slow movement as opposed to pursuing dreams of mushrooming wealth.

1. Review your Morals.

Examine the possibility that you will set attainable goals. Put each one down in your prosperity diary, introducing it with a sentence like this:

• Spending time with my kids at least once a day is essential to me.

• It's vital that my employer recognizes my abilities and that I am successful as a business owner.

• Having health insurance at my place of employment is vital to me. Finding a reliable source of residual income is crucial to me.

I value honesty, compassion, dependability, privacy, and relationships with my partner, spouse, and children.

A quiet workplace, receiving fair compensation for the work I do, and my relationship with my place of worship, my religion, and a higher power are all things I appreciate. Choose five unreachable statements from the list you have generated. Think of the statements as reflections of your core principles, which you will uphold no matter how challenging the situation may seem.

2. Set Long-Term Objectives.

Make a form similar to the one below, and list your objectives for the next five to ten years in the right-hand column. This form separates net worth from annual income.

It accounts for your available cash, the value of your possessions, and your debt and net worth target will be more thorough. If becoming a billionaire is your aim, you must have a million dollars in net worth instead of income.

Remember that investing, paying off debt, increasing savings, or acquiring expensive possessions can be matched as net worth.

3. Decide on immediate lifestyle goals

To advance toward achieving your long-term objectives, establish shorter-term milestones based on your answers to the following questions:

What steps should I take to accomplish my long-term non-financial goals? Which of these goals am I willing to focus on over the upcoming three months? To which of these am I ready to commit myself for the forthcoming year?

4. Set up yearly financial objectives

Record measurable one-year goals that help your long-term income and net worth objectives in your prosperity.

Be sure to update these goals as necessary at the end of each year. For instance, if your long-term plan is to double your net worth in seven years, your one-year goal might be to do so; during the following six years, you should aim to raise the percentage of gain each time.

Add concrete strategies for boosting your income and net worth in your one-year financial goals. Raising salaries, increasing corporate profits, and making investments with better yields are all potential ways to increase revenue.

5. Market and test your financial objectives.

Act as though you have already reached your financial goal. Consider that you have $50, and you start researching investing options while considering your options for extra funds. As you go, update your goals, replacing any inaccurate information.

Practise making investments after that. Pick a stock and start "paper trading," choosing how many shares to purchase at what price, monitoring, and ultimately determining when to sell it.

Consider buying a few stocks after your gains outweigh your losses.

Similarly, looking at homes in a price range can be beneficial.

What brand-new furniture would I need to buy? Is the neighbourhood safe according to my standards? How will having my children here influence them? Such questions may lead you to reevaluate your lifestyle objectives depending on your responses.

6. Common strategies for generating income.

Include trading time for money, as in a job or your service-oriented business; buying goods and selling them at a profit; and establishing sources of residual income such as investment from books, and income from rental properties.

Improve your position within the firm, or find a better job. Or you could supplement your job income by buying and selling products or building residual income.

Whichever approach you choose, it coincides with your values and will help you move toward your lifestyle goals. After deciding on a strategy, note any new skills or information you need to implement.

7. Imagine achieving your objectives.

You can make yourself more receptive to new prospects. Visualisations that include both mental imagery and associated emotions are the most powerful.

• Sit in a chair with your legs crossed at the ankles or flat on the floor and your hands softly resting on your lap.

Take a few deep breaths to help you concentrate, paying attention to your chest and abdomen as you inhale and exhale. Continue to breathe deeply while merely observing your thoughts, if it's active, without passing judgement.

Observing your thoughts, if it's active, without passing judgement.

• Once you feel at ease, let your breathing return to normal and visualise achieving one of your long-term financial or lifestyle objectives. Imagine yourself in this position of mastery, revelling in your accomplishments and spreading others' happiness, joy, or pride. Spend some time sitting with this thought and sensation.

• After that, speak your affirmations aloud while keeping your mouth shut, such as "I have accomplished my goal" or "I reside in the home of my dreams." Continue to visualise the experience of achieving your objective, the emotional states you desire.

You can add to the image as you like, Visualising the individuals you plan to share the finished product with. Bring your focus back whenever it wanders.

Creating Useful Ideas Regarding Money,

After limiting ideas have been located, replace them with constructive beliefs that further long-term goals. It's simple to change limiting beliefs by doubting their accuracy, examining how they contribute to your current identity, and dealing with your concerns about how new ideas can affect your life.

Be prepared to simultaneously let go of beliefs that prevent you from achieving your goals.

For instance, if you find out you believe "People like me never get rich," you may define what "people like me" are, then read biographies of people who have demonstrated these traits and succeeded financially, displacing your core belief. You may also think about how holding onto the limiting belief protects your identity, offers you an excuse to keep your current financial condition and prevents you from dealing with the impacts of change.

New insights and the identity factor. Because of the external changes that beliefs foster, particularly about behaviour, the Identity factor always becomes apparent. Uncertainty about what to anticipate or how to react can result in less confidence, indecision, and disorientation. The strength you need to create a new financial identity comes from anticipating these upheavals and reaching out to a prosperity buddy or other people who share your ideas.

CHAPTER 3

Form a Budget

Maintaining your budget with discipline can keep you organised. You won't be shocked by yearly expenses like auto insurance, which shows your cash flow.

Also, you won't be caught off guard by unforeseen costs because they have a place in a spending plan.

The two components of a budget are revenue and expenses.

Income is the cash you receive, including your salary, commission, dividends, interest earnings, child support, pension, or disability benefits. The money you are earning is not the things you must pay for are called expenses.

The rent or mortgage payment, the car payment, the phone bill, and the cost of homeowner's insurance are examples of fixed costs.

Food, petrol, entertainment, and clothing are a few variable costs.

Don't try to create a budget by cutting corners, guessing how much you'll spend, and then blaming the budget when it doesn't work because you utilised false information or failed to account for less frequent purchases (insurance, hockey fees, property taxes).

For budgeting, it is true. And if you're unwilling to put up the effort necessary to create a realistic budget and to adjust it as your circumstances change, Leave it alone! Examining your spending history is the most effective technique to determine your expenses.

Gather all regarding where your money has been spent, over the last six months, as each in the appropriate category, such as utilities, food, clothing, child care, and presents.

Add up the totals for each category, then divide the result by six. Your average for the month is that. Sum up all of them. That's how much money you've been using.

What to do is as follows: Buy a worksheet for your budget, and mortgage payments are necessary, while others, like cable and a cell phone. You might have to give up those nice-to-have items.

1. You must have a Savings Account. Pay off your debt, and an emergency fund. Till things improve, completely ignore saving.

2. A Decrease in Variable expenses Once more, certain things are essentially nice to have. You must eat, and you must be able to travel to work. Determine whether you can afford to eat organic food or take a taxi.

3. Focus on the Revenue.

You will need to make cuts if the budget still isn't balanced. Start by reducing the quantities for your variable expenses. Certain things you might need to get rid of; If you have debt, alcohol, cigarettes, mani-pedis, haircuts, coffee, lunch meals, and video games are all out of your price range.

You'll pay for everything, your participation in sports out of the entertainment budget. You can afford ground beef. Everyone should eat healthily, but to do so, you must exercise extreme caution, buy only seasonal foods, use coupons, and make every bite matter. And nobody is permitted to eat out!

4. Next, look at your fixed expenses. Reduce your phone, cable, and utility bills. Combine your home and auto insurance. Increase your deductible.

Reduce your insurance costs. When your only pair of winter boots stops functioning, there are moments when a piece of apparel crosses the line from good if you have children that will not stop growing.

In this instance, you add a must-have number to cover the essentials and then upgrade it to a nice-to-have number for all the extras you will desire. It's nice to have if you have to make cuts later.

5. Be Practical, not Create a Budget. if you cut back on a category to make the budget balance while fully aware that you will still need to spend. You're not being practical if you exclude clothing, household upkeep, recreation, family gifts, and auto repairs.

6. Be ready to change course quickly. Sometimes you have to spend money because crap happens. You may need to purchase new tires if your "vehicle repair" fund hasn't accrued enough to cover the expense.

Shortly, you "borrow" money from your home maintenance budget. The fact is that you cannot spend more money than you bring in. If you can't get the budget to balance, you must either make more money or eliminate expenses. One must pay back debt.

Also, put something aside for both the long-term and emergencies.

Good luck if you believe you can always make decisions on the go. Thank you for deciding to manage your financial future.

Make a balanced budget, and you've already made significant progress toward making your money work for you.

My budget is a holy book to me; it keeps me truthful. I can determine if my current expenses reflect a shift in my situation or whether I was not paying attention when I looked back at my previous spending.

My budget does not control me. I search for areas where I can cut back if I overindulge in entertainment for a month. I choose what to do.

Instead of being shocked by an unmanageable credit card bill, I'd much rather be aware that I'm over my vacation budget and make some modifications elsewhere.

CHAPTER 4

Cash Flow Management, A Cash Flow Budget: What Is It?

Timing is crucial when it comes to money. Individuals frequently find themselves with an extra week, paying many payments at once or splurging on fun things, only to run out the next day when they need to buy something essential.

And the estimate of how you will get and utilise cash and other financial resources is a cash flow budget. differs from a standard budget because it incorporates the timing of your revenue and expenses in dollar amounts for each line item. You can pinpoint your monthly shortfalls with a cash flow budget.

You can use it to have enough money to pay for the most crucial costs, such as rent, and avoid running out of money. You can effectively target areas for a cash flow budget. It can assist you in projecting and planning methods for distributing your money over the months when you don't have any. Budgeting for cash flow. There are three steps to creating a cash flow budget:

1. Recording your income and outgoing expenses for a week, two weeks, or a month.

2. Review your expenditures.

3. Establishing a cash flow budget using this data. A cash flow calendar. Setting goals for how you will use your revenue in the future is the focus of your cash flow budget.

To Avoid a Tax Bill, Compute Your Taxes

No, I'm not referring to submitting your tax return on time.

I'm referring to a clear understanding of your tax obligations so that you may ensure the proper amount and avoid receiving a tax bill.

When calculating how much income you should be paying in taxes, it doesn't matter if you have a second job, are on maternity or parental leave, or are earning money from other sources.

Make sure your taxes aren't your employer's responsibility, nor is it the responsibility of the government or the banking institution.

Don't forget that you'll need to repeat this computation if your maternity leave lasts more than two calendar years.

No matter where you get your money, you need to ensure that you're saving enough for taxes and don't get stuck with a payment that makes your finances difficult.

Avoid Tithing If You Owe Money

Do you tithe or give to charities while having debt? Stop giving; that isn't your money.

As long as it makes you happy, I have nothing against giving money. Choose because it is your money. You must pay for it, though.

Regarding tithes and charity donations, that is where I draw the line. You shouldn't be giving the tenth if it isn't your money.

As a result, I have an issue paying tithes when I have debt.

For those who feel they must tithe because it is an essential component of their worldview and who they are, it's time to start putting aside your pleasures and needs to give.

Say no to the coffee, the vacation, and the new sweater. Spend money with heartfelt generosity. If a sacrifice is necessary, then so be it. It necessitates planning out your financial strategy.

Tithing your own money is impossible if you have debt. Lenders from all over the world profiting greatly from your donation are supporting your "gift." Living within your means is a sign of responsible living.

You do not have the right to tithe to ease your conscience. Only financially stable people are allowed to tithe.

Tithing at the exact proportion and then using a monthly amount of your credit line is hypocritical because you are not donating.

Then you must tithe using your resources. Money need not be involved in sharing. You could talk about your experience.

You can exchange your possessions, even all the items purchased in debt. What would you be willing to give up for someone else to have?

Saving While Paying Off Your Debt

It's critical to pay off debt. But so too is developing a saving habit. Finding financial stability only requires one stage in the process.

You will be out of money if you don't take a balanced approach to your finances. Use your additional cash to pay off debt until you are completely debt-free.

Prioritising being debt-free over maintaining financial stability is crucial. Of course, you want to be debt-free forever. It requires planning. And balance is necessary.

Making decisions and committing to the detriment of other aspects of your financial life is foolish. When things start to go south, you'll use credit if you don't start saving for emergencies. Without investing, put off developing a highly beneficial habit. Is there ever a good moment to start saving money?

Now is the ideal day to start saving! And if doing that requires you to save $1 per day, then be it.

Start by not sacrificing the other components of your financial plan, such as your goals, spending plan, emergency fund, insurance, and estate plan, to pay off your debt as quickly as feasible.

Get a second job, a third job, and pay off the debt if you're serious about doing so and want it to happen quickly. Break your ass. Don't give up your savings.

Saving

We can establish good habits! Make saving a lifestyle. Pay yourself first, as the proverbial classic says. Pay yourself a portion of your paycheck every time before you do anything else.

Before paying the rest of the bills, treat yourself first and tell yourself you deserve the money.

Examine your spending in detail as well. Cut off any item or product that proves superfluous and handle your life like any other would treat his business.

Just storing up the money you would have spent on a daily $4 coffee and forgoing it would start to pile up over time.

Some people manage their finances carefully. People are more likely to be self-centred and have no desire to help others.

Must we spend? Obviously, to keep the money in circulation. Furthermore, if we don't fully appreciate life, If debt collectors are continuously calling, we want to be able to enjoy life.

I can attest that they can be incredibly bothersome. With material possessions, a portion of what we buy is unnecessary and adds little to no value to our lives.

Dealing with Debt, What is Debt

You have debt if you borrow money from a person or a company. When you owe money, you must repay it, occasionally through scheduled instalments.

You frequently make those payments using funds from your upcoming paycheck.

While borrowing money may allow you to obtain something immediately, you may have ongoing monthly obligations for several months or even years.

Credit differs from debt. The capacity to borrow money is credit, credit results in debt. You can get credit without owing money. For instance, you might possess a credit card with no balance.

Debt: Is It Good or Bad?

You can build assets for the future or achieve your ambitions by taking on some debt.

Individuals frequently claim that taking debt to finance your education, a dependable car, a start-up business, or the purchase of a home is the use of debt.

But things aren't always that easy. A certification or degree, for instance, may lead to a better-paying job and increased job stability, so borrowing money to enhance your education may be a wise use of debt.

But, instead of advancing your ambitions, student debt will hold you back if you take on the debt but fail to complete the certificate or degree.

You can keep moving in the right direction and achieve your objectives by taking a loan for a dependable car to bring you to and from work.

The risk of owning more than one car is worth it if you borrow 100% of its value.

Also, you won't have as much money for other expenses if you purchase a Car which costs more than you need.

It may motivate you to go to work, but it might also prevent you from achieving your financial objectives.

A loan to launch a business could help you and others earn money. But, if the company fails, you can find yourself in a position where you owe money but don't have any sources of revenue.

A loan to purchase your home may be a strategy to achieve your objectives.

Nevertheless, if you can't make the payments on time or you wind up owing more than your house is worth, that debt could cause you to fall behind financially for a very long time.

We're not trying to terrify you with this information.

Debt that many people regard as "positive" should be addressed cautiously.

Credit card debt, payday loans, and pawn loans are all examples of loans that some individuals see as "bad" debt, and is because they include fees and interest and do not help when used for things you consume, such as dining out, buying gifts, or taking a vacation.

Yet you can find a means to pay them back the debt to assist you in filling a cash flow gap.

Hence, no debt type is "good" or "bad." Understanding your objective or your demand for this reason.

Before making your final purchase decision, you can shop for the credit you require, especially for purchases like a car or a home. The debt secured or unsecured is another method to comprehend debt. Debt with an asset tied to it is secured debt.

If you don't pay your loan, You can record all your bills on a debt management worksheet and categorise them as secured or unsecured.

The debt-to-income ratio is a more accurate approach to assessing debt.

Your monthly debt payments are compared to your gross monthly income before taxes and other deductions to get your debt-to-income ratio.

You may determine how much of your income is spent on debt by looking at the resulting percentage. A percentage indicates that you may not be as financially secure as you would be since you have less money to cover other expenses.

Everything else refers to your non-debt requirements, wants, and commitments.

Preventing Debt Traps

It is crucial to stay out of debt if you're borrowing money to cover an urgent necessity. When people get into a debt trap, they take out new loans to cover the payments on their original loans.

The reason it is a trap is that it can be challenging for many people to break free from the cycle of borrowing money and accruing additional debt to make their loan payments while also having money left over for other needs like food, rent, and transportation.

CHAPTER 5

Recognizing One's Financial Condition and Spending Patterns

First, you should look at your monthly spending patterns and classify them. You have two options for this: manually or with the budgeting applications.

These will offer you a solid basis for where you are right now and assist you in creating a budget for the future.

Reduce Idling Expense

Creating your budget may take some time, but it will be worthwhile once you realise which areas of spending are unnecessary.

Do you have any subscriptions, for instance, that you may have allowed lapsing? Describe any goods or services you no longer utilise.

One of the things you can do to improve your financial performance and health is to decrease costs.

1. Specify Attainable Objectives For Your Savings. Consider long-term objectives.

It makes no difference! Setting and maintaining goals is most important. For your newly discovered shorted financial success, doing so can have some benefits.

It may increase your motivation to make financial sacrifices.

When you handle your money well, you may gradually increase your confidence, whether saving for a home or another "big ticket" item that won't fit daily...

On the other hand, we advise against starting too big.

In the first month, choose goals and spending limits that are simple to meet; once you've accomplished your objective, increase the amount in the next month.

2. Repay Any Debts You Can.

It's easier to say than to pay off debts early. It might be challenging to manage your finances to accrue interest over time. It might be prudent to utilise any money you have saved to pay off your obligations to prevent future increases in interest.

3. Establish Savings Accounts.

Creating savings accounts is among the simplest ways to manage your finances. You'll divide your savings among several budgets.

When you are getting paid, you can put money into these pots and wait to access it until you've met your savings target. You can do this monthly or weekly.

Another tool banks provide is to transfer any balance from your current account at the end of the month.

4. Keep Tabs On Your Expenses

The most important thing you can do to improve your money management is to keep track of your spending because most of the time.

Many takeout meals each month makes it simple to go over budget! You may manage your finances and keep track of your expenditures in a few different ways.

You can try saving receipts to enter your budget, keep track of your expenses in a notebook or notes app, or even incorporate your bank account information into tracking software.

5. Remember to Take Care of Yourself.

While trying to manage your finances better and make improvements, motivation is essential. We advise sticking to your budget.

Set up a separate savings account that serves as a "Slush Fund" and use it to deposit any extra funds left over after other expenses and payments.

6. Shop Around for the Best Deals.

Another money management and budgeting technique that frequently aids people in improving their financial situation is to shop around for the deal.

Whether buying a car or items like groceries, you can do this by using price comparison websites.

Also, you can register for programs that trawl search for deals or find less expensive options for the goods and services you buy used items. Have a peek at your credit report at number.

7. A record of your borrowing and timely debt repayment on file in your credit history. Your credit score is probably good if you have never been behind on your loan obligations. Your creditworthiness will be evaluated by creditors using this score, which is a numerical value.

Conclusion

Your financial situation might not be as bad as you believe if you grasp it. Or not. You might be eking out a win if the number is small.

You get paid more frequently than you do with spending. You most likely receive payment once per week, twice per week, or once per month, yet you still spend money every day, don't you? Your perspective on money becomes distorted as a result, which makes wasting money.

For a month, make a list of every purchase you make with cash, a debit card, or a credit card to obtain a better understanding of how much money you waste.

The same thing should be done by your partner or spouse.

Every time you leave the house, keep a tiny notebook with you so you can record every expense straight away rather than trying to recall it later.

www.ingramcontent.com/pod-product-compliance
Lightning Source LLC
Chambersburg PA
CBHW071144220526
45467CB00015B/1844